Breathing
is my
Superpower

Alicia Ortego

This Superpower
belongs to

This book is dedicated to adults and little ones,
to all grandparents, daughters, and sons.
This book is dedicated to all fathers and mothers,
from the youngest to the oldest, sisters, and brothers.
This book is dedicated to all kids, clumsy or naughty;
to those sleepy, shy, curious, and those on a potty;
to all twins or triplets, and quadruplets too.
In other words, this book is dedicated to **YOU**!

My name is Sofia, and this is my unicorn, **Bee**.
She is seven years old too and special like **me**.

I love fairies
and magical creatures and **stories**.

I'm usually happy
but sometimes I have **worries**.

I'm afraid to sleep
with the lights off at **night**,

because some dreams
have monsters with teeth, sharp and **white**.

I feel upset when other kids
don't play with **me**.

On those days I am as angry
as angry can **be**.

I asked my mom why I felt this,
not once but **twice**.

She was understanding
and had some good **advice**.

"When you are upset, and you don't know what to **do**,
try *Five Breathing* exercise, it is sure to help **you**.

Stretch one of your hands out like a big shining **star**,
and trace your fingers like you're driving a toy **car**.

Slide up each finger while breathing in through your **nose**.
Feel the air fill your body from your head to your **toes**.

Slide down the other side with the finger of your other **hand**.
Breathe out through your mouth and you will soon feel calm. **Understand**"

My mommy always knows best. She is so smart and **wise**.
So, I decided to try this fun *Five Breathing* **exercise**.

The next day at school, when the teacher called my **name**,
I had to read my homework, but I felt fear and **shame**.

I started deep breathing: one breath in, one breath **out**.
Wow! This exercise works well, there is no **doubt**.

My friend didn't want to play with me
that day at **school**.

So, I took five slow deep breaths
and felt calm and **cool**.

When I got home, my mom made me an egg to **eat**.

I don't like eggs, so I started stamping my **feet**.

Then I remembered that slow, deep breathing **good**.
I stretched out my hand, breathed in and out, and then ate my **food**.

I used to shout a lot, throw things, and stamp my **feet**.
Now I like eggs more than cookies or other **sweets**.

I use *Five Breathing* exercise
when I'm upset or **sad**.

I slide over my fingers
when I feel angry and **mad**.

Last night, when I put on my pajamas, soft and **red**,
I used the exercise before going to **bed**.

I stretched out one hand just like a big shining **star**.
One breath in, one breath out, like I'm driving a toy **car**.

After breathing,
I was no longer afraid of the **dark**.

Instead of monsters,
I dreamed of a fun aqua **park**.

I decided that stress would never ruin my **day**.
With my mom's advice, I stay calm and ready to **play**.

Nothing can stop me,
not a broken toy or a rain **shower**.

I'll tell you a secret —
breathing is my **superpower**!

Bonus!
Breathing Exercise Cards.

Bubble Breathing

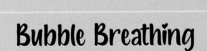

- ♥ Imagine you have a wand to blow bubbles
- ♥ Take a deep breath in through your nose to make a big bubble
- ♥ Exhale slowly through your mouth as if you are blowing a bubble through a wand.
- ♥ Great job! You just completed one deep breath!
- ♥ Repeat as many times as necessary

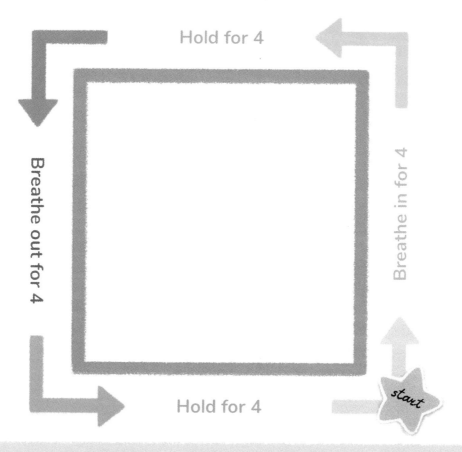

Hold for 4

Breathe in for 4

Breathe out for 4

Hold for 4

start

Square Breathing

- ♥ Start at the bottom right of the square
- ♥ Inhale slowly through your nose filling up your lungs, to the count of four as you trace the first side of the square
- ♥ Hold your breath for four counts as you trace the second side of the square
- ♥ Exhale slowly emptying the oxygen from your lungs to the count of four as you trace the third side of the square
- ♥ Hold your breath for four counts as you trace the final side of the square
- ♥ Great job! You just completed one deep breath!
- ♥ Repeat as many times as necessary

Lazy 8 Breathing

- ♥ Put your finger in the air and place it at the top of the number eight
- ♥ Inhale slowly while drawing the number eight in the air
- ♥ Once you get back to the top, slowly exhale as you trace the number eight again.
- ♥ Great job! You just completed one deep breath!
- ♥ Repeat as many times as necessary

Soup Breathing

- ♥ Imagine you have a bowl of hot yummy soup in your hands
- ♥ Take a slow breath in through your nose, smelling a soup
- ♥ Slowly breath out through your mouth to cool down the hot soup
- ♥ Great job! You just completed one deep breath!
- ♥ Repeat as many times as necessary

Dear reader,

Thank you for trusting me and reading my book. I would appreciate it if you would let me know your impressions. Please take two minutes and share your review on Amazon with the millions who are waiting for your feedback.

From the author:

This book was written for all children to help them connect their body with their feelings. We all sometimes feel upset and scared — and our children are no different. The best way to help each other is by sharing our experiences.

Breathing is My Superpower shows both children and adults *Five Breathing Technique*, the exercise that is fun and helpful at the same time. So, if you want to explain to your little ones how to deal with their negative emotions, use this cute book and put a smile on their face.

Alicia Ortego

BOOKS FOR KIDS

Breathing is My Superpower is the second book from *My Superpower Series* — the growth mindset books for kids, suitable for all ages as well as anyone who works with children.

Visit my website for more information and free printables. www.aliciaortego.com or scan the code below

Thank you again for your support!
— Alicia Ortego

Collect them all!

Made in the USA
Las Vegas, NV
07 April 2021